the anvil
of
ulster

an anthology of verse by monty alexander

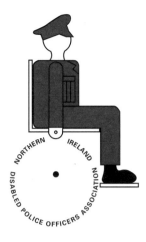

15th Anniversary
1983-1998

Our Association is always very grateful for the support we receive.
I hope you enjoy reading this book.

b. McDonaghy.

Chairman DPOA

Disabled Police Officers Association, PANI, Seapark, 151 Belfast Road,
Carrickfergus, Co. Antrim, BT38 8PL.
Telephone: (01232) 700719/700721 Fax: (01232) 700728
Internet: http://www.ruc.police.uk

Preface

The Northern Ireland Disabled Police Officers Association is a registered charity. Since it was established in 1983, the Association has aimed to improve the quality of life for officers who were seriously, or permanently disabled through terrorism.

In 1993 I introduced a programme for UTV, which highlighted the suffering of these people, long after the cameras have moved their gaze elsewhere. That broadcast was a graphic illustration of the on-going plight of men, and women, who are coping with their disabilities. It won a National Television Award in London in 1995, and after seeing the programme again, the Author of this anthology decided to donate his poems, offering his work for publication.

The proceeds from this book will help the DPOA. It is a worthy cause.

Paul Clark

ACKNOWLEDGEMENTS

Special thanks to Paul CLARK of Ulster Television for writing the
'Foreword' of this book.

For their support in the publication of this anthology.
Mr Charles McCONAGHY, QPM, Chairman of the DPOA.
Mrs Hazel McCREADY, Secretary of the DPOA.
Mr Sam MALCOLMSON, BEM, Former Chairman of the DPOA
and Committee Members of the Association.

ALSO THANKS TO

Mr Brian MALCOLMSON, for sketches in respect of certain poems.
Mr James LAVERY, who designed the cover and wrote the profile of the Author.
Miss Elaine McCLURE, of the 'Ulster Society', for help in publishing.
Mr Kenneth ANDERSON, of the Ulster Folk and Transport Museum,
for the photograph featured on the front cover.
Mr Kenneth LUNN for his preparation to print.

All the proceeds from the sale of this publication, is for the
Northern Ireland Disabled Police Officers Association,
being a registered charity, to help in their endeavours to relieve suffering.

ISBN 0 9532614 0 9

Printed by
Northern Whig Ltd., 107 Limestone Road, Belfast

The Author

Hugh Montgomery 'Monty' Alexander, was born in the town of Lisburn, Northern Ireland, on the 30th May 1943, to parents, Hugh and Agnes Alexander. Their home was at Purdysburn Village, near Belfast. His Father, born at Ballydown, in the County of Down, was a mechanical engineer and his Mother, from Ballylesson, also in the County of Down, was a linen weaver before marriage. Monty grew up with a great awareness of industrial Ulster and when his schooling was over, firstly at Purdysburn Village School, Botanic Primary School, Belfast, and finally Oranges Civil Service Academy, Chapel Lane, Belfast, he followed his Father's footsteps into engineering.

In 1968, he made a career change, joining the Royal Ulster Constabulary, serving in many areas of Northern Ireland, until retiring in March 1997.

In writing his poetry, Monty has drawn on his formative years, growing up in village surroundings at Purdysburn and his association with Ballydown, following the 1939-45 war. His family moved to Belfast and he spent his teenage and early adult life in that City. His attendance at Oranges Academy, being a religiously mixed school, but predominately Catholic, gave him an understanding of the diverse cultures in Northern Ireland. His employment in engineering and later as a Police Officer, also contributed to this anthology. His late Father was an influence, having also been adroit with verse.

The Author is blessed with a mind which retentively records all that he witnesses, either by sight, sound or personal experience. Additionally he has the capability to transcribe such to verse, for others pleasure and enjoyment.

Verse is a gift, like music and Monty crosses the divide in Ulster, giving no offence to any class or creed. One can step inside his poetry and wear the mantle as if oneself had penned it.

In his lifetime, Monty Alexander has courted death and danger and conversely has experienced joyful camaraderie, with the public and in Police service.

This anthology of verse, some of which has already gained acclaim, truly reflects his inner feelings for a Province, battered and shaped by its inhabitants and no doubt led to his chosen title, 'The Anvil Of Ulster'.

JIMMY LAVERY

The Author has received the following acknowledgements and awards for individual poems he has written.

Personal letter from Mr Bill Clinton, President of the USA.

Personal letter from Mr Tony Blair, Prime Minister of Great Britain.

Personal letter from Mr Chris Patten, The Last Governor of Hong Kong.

Poems published in National Anthologies of Verse in 1995, 1996 and 1997.

1997 National Open Competition - Award of Excellence from 'Poetry in Print', for the poem, 'A Casualty of War', featured in this publication.

Index

Living Reminders

On a day preparing to travel east, to visit London Town
I saw a group of people, who made me stop and frown
They sat silently awaiting, a chariot of the sky
To their invited destination, they were with me to fly

Engrossed to know just who they were, I started to enquire
About this band of injured souls, whose suffering is so dire
What I was told in reply, made me shed a tear
They'd been upholders of the Law, in a land of fear

On this soil they did their duty and managed to survive
In spite of bomb and bullet, some barely still alive
There was a time when able, they went forth to face the foe
Protecting all and sundry, until the assassin laid them low

Not for them the door of death, but a lifetime filled with pain
Theirs to lie or sit a'wondering, if it was all in vain
They know if they had died, with marchers behind the hearse
Preacher men would have lamented, with others reciting verse

Sometimes they muse and daydream, on this funeral not meant to be
Visualising all the attenders, including those of high degree
If some of these imagined people, would call just now and then
Unable to make a visit, they could always use the pen

So spare a thought for these souls, whose suffering is immense
A reward for doing their duty, including your defence
The limbless, scarred and twisted, those who cannot see
Held the line and faced the threat, on this side of the Irish Sea

Sometimes they have the feeling, better if they had just died
Sparing a lot of embarrassment, with everything cut and dried
But they bravely soldier on, facing the daily grind
Reflecting on when young and fit, patrolling with their kind

Then from a London Policeman, a suggestion sound and plain
Form your own association, to help the disabled and those in pain
And this is exactly what was done, so they would not be deprived
This remnant of the victims, who have tenaciously survived

21.6.96

The Stone

Encased within that antique throne

Is an older ancient stone

A symbol of our identity

Laid down by God's decree

Of our breeding and our line

At the end of time a sign

To all the doubters, maybe thee

Who live here and across the sea

On this rock, Jacob laid his head

As he dreamed upon his bed

Looking up that heavenly stair

He saw Jehovah standing there

The Lord did him and his anoint

To carry his blessing from that point

Your descendants as the dust will be

And nations will be blessed through thee

I will protect you where'er you are

My glory will be your guiding star

Waking in terror on that sacred sod

Jacob called it, 'Bethel' - House of God

There erecting his pillow, stone of destiny

As a memorial pillar, for all to see

27.4.96

A Tribute

Groomsport is a little town

On the coast of County Down

I often sit on its harbour wall

Listening to the seagulls call

I hear the waves lap the shore

At other times they're a crashing roar

I then will rest within the lee

And watch the foam backed angry sea

In the habitat of the human race

This coast must have a special place

On the waters I see unfold

Heroic dramas perhaps untold

When Groomsport men sailed the seven seas

On wooden ships in all degrees

Others answered the patriotic call

And in foreign fields did fall

Above the harbour is an obelisk

Reminding us of sacrifice and risk

So that here we can always be

In little Groomsport by the sea

3.3.95

The Dawn

Looking out from Erin's Isle
As the east wind blows

Frothing water on the rocks
The inward tide flows

Sound of rollers breaking
With intermittent rush

Anchored seaweed clinging
As jagged cauldrons flush

The morning light emerging
Unveils a tempestuous sea

Night's mantle is receding
Flitting shadows flee

Profiled afar a passing ship
At junction of Earth and sky

Above Nature's roar I hear
A gull's piercing cry

Alternating wind and tide
Upon this northern shore

From beyond the dawn of 'Man'
Countless million times before

27.10.96

The Homecoming of William Francis Black

Army No. 13119776

The year was nineteen forty six
As we sat on the close at the hill
Awaiting the arrival from Palestine
Of my favourite Uncle Bill

We heard the grind of the engine
In that bus all battered and worn
Bringing Billy back to his kinfolk
And the cot where he was born

Our eyes were transfixed on the Hollow
Along the flat of the road
Standing there to the front of the cottage
Which was my Granny's abode

The bus then pulled in at the Churchyard
Of Ballylesson, known as 'Drumbo'
A whistle alerted old 'Darkie' the dog
And down the hill he did go

Years had passed, but the dog still knew
That clarion call of old
As he ran to see his Master
The returning Warrior Bold

We cheered as he came to the cross-roads
With kitbag held on the shoulder
Wearing boots under gaiters and battledress
The garb of every soldier

Then that canine bundle collided with him
As the kitbag was flung to the ground
Yelping, laughter and barking
Were the sounds to be heard all around

Grandfather at toil on the hillside
Stepped out and away from the plough
A hand raised to fend off the sunlight
He watched from under his brow

Enthralled and enraptured to see him
The dog pranced about at his feet
As Billy walked up the 'Loanin'
Anxious for us to meet

Granny went forward to greet him
As she hugged, the beret fell from his head
She thanked God for the return of her youngest
The son who could have been dead

After this there was talk and rejoicing
With many a tale to tell
Then from the Church, as if in salute to the brave
I heard the toll of the Belfry Bell

1.1.97

The Trolley Bus Run

In Belfast Town away long ago
Trolleybuses ferried people to and fro

To board a Trolley, you went to the back
And then just stepped onto the deck

I would sit on the seat beside the door
Where there was a pole, from roof to floor

It was nice to sit quietly at the rear
To see the people and at them peer

Now Trolleybuses had no doors to slide
And you could get on, from back or side

There was a Shipyard man, called Sammy Minter
A hard worker and natural sprinter

He always managed the Trolley to miss
As it sped off with a swishing hiss

Now Minter would come up, from the rear
Running through the traffic, devoid of fear

Duncher on his head, cocked to the side
With his stocky legs, opening wide

As the Trolley moved faster and faster
You'd swear that he would meet disaster

Running full pelt, with his head flung back
Supported on his bull size neck

His hob-nailed boots would smash the ground
Over the Trolley swish, they were the only sound

As the Trolley veered around Cleaver's corner
I'd watch and swear he was a 'goner'

Sparks would fly from beneath each boot
As out of Donegall Place he'd shoot

Then with one almighty angled dive
In a superhuman effort, to survive

He'd reach straight out and grab the pole
His body following, in lopsided roll

With precision landing, right on the deck
Then saunter to his seat, without looking back

I'd watch him, piece box under his arm
Thinking, the Lord kept him free from harm

Then I would wonder and quietly reflect
With his strength and agility, I did suspect

Olympic athletes, compared to him were tame
He could have beaten them all and taken the fame

All it required, was a Trolley up ahead
For Sammy round the track to sped

20.2.96

Reflections

A moment or two with the Constabulary Gazette
Can sometimes fill you with regret
Faces of young men long ago
Who now are gone, or old and slow
These were the giants of yesteryear
Within their rank, or sporting sphere
They were men, who in black were dressed
Tunics to the neck and trousers pressed
Boots shone up, with soles hob-nailed
Whatever their task, they never failed
They did not stop, or call retreat
But continued forth, with ponderous beat
Always tall, looking quietly mean
You often wondered, where they had been
Some wore ribbons from bygone wars
Having served as soldiers, or jack tars
From shipyard, office and farm they came
Their purpose in joining, was always the same
Upholding everything that was right
And if required, to stand and fight
With belligerent purpose and directed skill
On all those opposing, their concerted will
In photographs, I see the faces
From forgotten stations and sporting places
Matt Nelson of high hurdle fame
He's still about and just the same
Davy Davidson putting the shot
At the Commonwealth Games, he was on the spot
Jimmy Nesbitt was friend of many
Throwing the discus, he was better than any
Bob Agar on the rugby field
He was a stalwart and didn't yield
Bruno Moore, never afraid to box
Either in the ring, or at the docks
These are all men that I have known
Their retirements and passing I do bemoan
But the Gazette, keeps our memories good
Reminding us that we stand, where those men stood

2.2.95

11

The Cries of Belfast 1981

The Constable on his daily round

The sound he hears when on the ground

The early morn with its cloak of grey

The City Hall birds chirping away

The Milkmen crash and shunt about

The Bus Inspectors wave their arms and shout

The Workers answer the factory horn

The odd one wonders, is this why they were born

The tattoo beat, of office girls heels

The engines grunt and braking squeals

The rain comes down and slaps the street

The result is the sound, of running feet

The children suddenly released from school

The only thing in their heads, to act the fool

The high pitched screech, of the Police siren

The look of fear, where joy has been

The Wellington Place, with the bomb to blow

The traffic has all but ceased to flow

The explosion then, with its flash so bright

The trailing thunder, causes great fright

The daylight gone, people homeward bound

The streets are cleared, of scrap and sound

The hour of midnight, soon draws near

The people look forward, to another year

The ships in the Harbour, blast their horns

The New Year comes, whilst 'Father Time' scorns

1982

Avarice

When I was young I spent my days
Beside the River Bann
As it meandered through County Down
Along its banks I ran

Or I would sit upon a knoll
And with great patience wait
For that elusive king sized fish
To take my subtle bait

Then I grew up and wandered off
To countries great and far
Wherever there was money
That was my guiding star

I dug for gold in mountain chains
Near California's shore
I cursed the Sun for going down
Because I wanted more

With Hotentots I traded beads
For treasures they knew not
In single minded purpose
What I pursued, I got

I smuggled every item
And contraband by the ton
Sometimes from the Revenue Man
I had to cut and run

I have achieved my purpose
And accumulated spoil
But was it really worth the effort
For my soul to soil

From my palatial home
Within this foreign clime
I think back to Erin's Isle
In another sphere of time

That was when I had real wealth
On the revolving wheel of fate
Not as I sit old and gray
Contemplating my estate

17.3.96

Hallowe'en

Its the thirty first of October
In the coming of the year
The night is full of witches
And the people full of fear

On looking up above
One might see a few Banshees
Screaming and a'howlin'
As they wind among the trees

Warlocks, ghosts and spectres
Will fill you full of dread
And no one wants to wander far
In case they meet the dead

If you were out in the dark
And met someone from the past
They could be a demon
And a spell on you might cast

We pride ourselves among other things
In being a hardy race
And say there is no danger
We cannot safely face

Remembering 'Oul Wives'tales
That as a child we heard
Rattlin' chains could remind us
And you'd be really scared

On reflection I'll just sit here
And await the break of day
Then with my fears behind me
I'll be on my way

20.10.95

Derry

August was the month, back in sixty nine
Tempers they were rising, the weather being fine
It was there we stood in the riot line

Near the banks of the River Foyle

Police had come from far and near
A parade through that City to steer
Then confrontation, devastation and fear

Londonderry was on the boil

In their advance, protesters smashed and burned
There was debris and wreckage wherever you turned
In the search to destroy, nothing was spurned

On that restless ancient soil

The hatred and venom had to be seen
As they attacked those wearing the tartan green
Intent to offend and the law demean

From their task they didn't recoil

And so it continues year by year
As politicians to past and future peer
With each generation another to rear

On the banks of the River Foyle

14.8.96

The Belfast Engineer

It is the town where I was born
Within green rolling hills
A place of thriving industry
And resplendent red bricked mills

As I have wrought, in this foreign clime
Where the temperature is high
I think back to Belfast Town
Where the gantries touch the sky

I see great ships I worked upon
That later sailed the seas
In tempest, typhoon, ocean storms
And gentle coastal lees

A contribution to the World
Has been the Belfast Engineer
Men of substance and resource
With metal their career

Is Mackies Foundry still up there
On the Springfield Road
Producing looms to weave the jute
At an Indian abode

And does the Sirocco still prepare
Machines for 'Darjeeling Tea'
At that busy junction
Where the Lagan meets the sea

What about the slipways
Are the boats still sliding down
Built by Harland and Wolff
For shippers of renown

Are the 'Linen Barons' happy
With their produce on the loom
Or has the lack of orders
Filled them with gloom and doom

Do the 'Head Line' boats still ply
Those North Atlantic Lanes
Going up the Great Lakes
To bring home the prairie grains

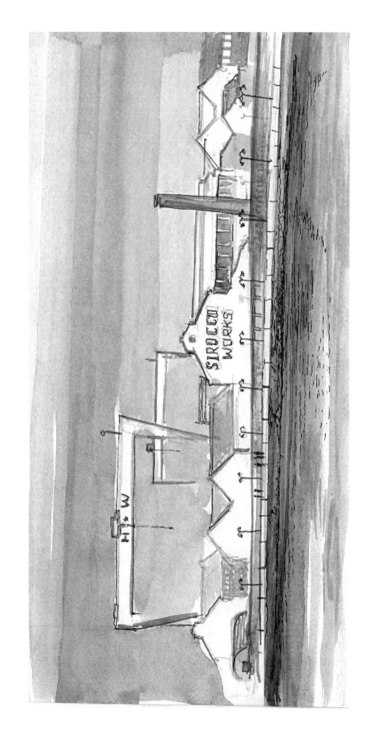

Are Short and Harland still making
Their miracles of the air
And reassuring their customers
They'll be able to supply a spare

Forty years or more have passed
Since I left that busy scene
Pursuing engineering work
Where far off fields looked green

It is with pride I now reflect
On that crucible of inventive skills
Nestling in the Lagan's vale
Between those green banked hills

28.2.96

A Moment

In my dreams I see a place

Which in my memory I can trace

Within a vale on Erin's Isle

On a road beside a stile

Overlooking a field of golden corn

Leading to the cot where I was born

It was just there in noon's full glare

I fell bewitched by her auburn hair

She walked as straight as any rush

The grass her feet did gently brush

To speak I could not find my tongue

I was shy and very young

She simply smiled on gliding by

Her eyes the blue of a summer sky

Each like a delicate 'Forget-me not'

Enraptured I stood upon that spot

Watching her perfect form depart

Whilst Cupid's arrows struck my heart

From whence she came, I do not know

And after her I did not go

In all my wanderings beyond the foam

I still dream of my Irish home

To me that Colleen is still there

Young and fresh, with her auburn hair

2.3.96

Dedicated to the Members of the Royal Ulster Constabulary and the Royal Ulster Constabulary Reserve.

Lest We Forget

Law Enforcers whose role is vital
Have proudly held the Royal title
It has been their duty, to go forth and serve
This Land of Ours, with courage and nerve

Out of office, farm and industry
Others came from across the sea
Facing sniper, bomb and blast
When the terror dice was cast

They did not have to question why
Knowing the risk, that they might die
Upholding the law, was their only rule
Some were young and straight from school

Thus this calling, was the reason
To face the killer, death and treason
The assassin with his evil tools
Not a task for errant fools

Grenade or bullet, in day or night
Could kill a man, or rob the sight
Of those who chose to answer the call
Shining examples, to one and all

Serving in County, Town and City
The terrorist for them, devoid of pity
Always knowing, wherever sent
The murderer waited, with intent

To injure, maim, or take a life
Promoting their cause and bitter strife
Careful never themselves to show
When venturing forth to strike a blow

Not for them to wear, the uniform of green
Or any other, so as not to be seen
Unlike the Royal Ulster, who always walk tall
Custodians of Law and protectors of all

20.1.97

The Mary Dell

Having served my penal yoke
I stood a Felon freed

Seven years and transportation
The Judge he had decreed

An older man and wiser
My thoughts they were of home

As I gazed at the Tasman Sea
With its ribbons of frothing foam

I could see breakers crashing
In another hemisphere

Around an island people
Far away and nowhere near

It was just then I saw her
A square rigger on the swell

Her Master wanted crewmen
She was called the Mary Dell

On seeking out the Agent
I agreed to join the crew

No money to be paid me
Only passage home in lieu

The Agent looked me straight in the eye
And spat upon the ground

I could see him thinking
Unblinking he made no sound

Then he asked if I knew the ship
Being the Mary Dell

Bound for home, but not for some
She was known as the Barque from Hell

Her Master, once a slaver
Cursed to the core of his soul

Incited by the call of profit
Delivering cargo, his only goal

The figurehead was a Siren fair
Arms stretched like a bird in flight

Mouth open wide in silent scream
Her eyes burning bright

So I went and climbed aboard
With others of my kind

And before the black eyed Master
Eighty three crewmen, we were lined

I am the Captain here he said
We'll sail without delay

Any man found slacking
His back I'll surely flay

Seeing him with speckled beard
And eyes like coals at night

I could sense the iron within him
A friendless chilling sight

With windlass turned and anchor stowed
He gave order to make sail

Surveying all before him
Leaning over the bowsprit rail

That penal shore behind me
I felt like a man reborn

But unbeknown to some aboard
Ahead of us lay the Horn

For a week or two, plain sailing
Was the order of the day

Until the storm and tempest came
With Neptune in the fray

Whipped and abused by sharpened wind
The Master cursed and damned us all

Pulling canvas to the yardarm
I saw three Mariners fall

Pitched and thrown upon the wave
Was that accursed ship

By all the power, of the Gods
That held us in its grip

Worse still to be, we faced the Horn
That cauldron of angry water

Where I saw the mainmast split
Like a musket, I heard it shatter

Many a man went overboard
Never seen, or to return

In hatred we cursed the Master
That he in Hell would burn

Then we left that Cape behind
Sailing north on a safer sea

A triumphant battered spectre
No longer, crewmen eighty three

As we disembarked at Plymouth
I saw him standing there

The black eyed poisoned Master
Watching me, with malignant stare

A shiver ran along my spine
Leaving that Mary Dell

As I glanced to the figurehead
The Siren out of Hell

23.11.96

Purdysburn River

When just an inquisitive little boy, I would watch the Burn

With innocent fascination, from it I could not turn

I noted the size and angle, of every protruding rock

Some of them were mountain tops, or harbours for ships to dock

Not to skirt the river, was my Mother's rule

Without her ever knowing, I'd skip to a sheltered pool

There watching bugs and beetles, on that little pond

But it was the sticklebacks, of which I was really fond

Looking back to that time, away in the days of yore

As a man I had an urge, to see that Burn once more

And there it was still running, that simple little stream

Just as it has always been, in my thoughts and dream

Those mountain tops and harbours, are still in place just there

With descendants of earlier sticklebacks, inside their watery lair

Many things upon this World, have really changed a lot

But everything is just the same, at that beauty spot

13.5.96

The Bomb Call

The call would come when the time was right

Made when the Bomber was well out of sight

Five, ten or fifteen minutes to go

You had to be fast and never slow

Clearing the area, a Policeman's concern

Over the years, many lessons to learn

Get the people to leave, or push them out

Having to cajole, scream, yell or shout

A bomb with the timer ticking away

Nobody could be allowed to stay

And all the time, the thought was there

The Bomber was a person, who didn't care

If the explosion, were to kill or maim

A blow for the cause, just the same

10.12.95

In Consideration Of My Friend

AHMED HASSAY

I met an unbeliever, accepting just what he'd seen
The trees, the sky, the water, places where he had been

Show me your God, Jehovah and like you I will believe
Said I, this I cannot do, but before you take your leave

Reflect on things you do not see, yet we know they're there
Sounds you hear, what we feel and don't forget the air

The God for whom you search, is with you all around
Walking the Earth along with you and growing on the ground

Also consider the life existing, in the wave below
Going about its business, in a place you cannot go

Bear in mind the birds that fly, in air we just can't see
I hope you are convinced my friend, listening to this plea

Then I met a Moslem, a darker man than I
An Egyptian of the Nile, from beneath a burning sky

He talked to me of Allah, living miracles that he knew
A man of balanced wisdom, with a reasoned point of view

We considered Pyramids, the Sphinx and many other things
Including those hidden places, in the Valley Of The Kings

He spoke reverently of this Earth, and its life unique
Enraptured with the mysteries, to solve, his mind did seek

From an ancient culture, contained in the shifting sand
This quiet Son of Ishmael, spoke of his native land

Here was a man of different creed, a different creed than I
But here was a man of similar view, on whom I could rely

You see, Allah that he spoke of, the creator of everything
Is your and my Jehovah, of whom the faithful sing

2.7.96

From the foundation of the British Army, Irishmen have formed
an integral part, in every rank. One who followed this path was
Nathaniel JEST of Belfast, a third generation soldier.
He enlisted in the 1st Battalion, The King's Regiment (Liverpool) at Armagh,
on the 14th September 1925 - Army No 3765052.
After having served in Malta, Sudan, Egypt and India,
he was seriously wounded, with loss of limb, in the retreat to
Dunkirk, 1940, having been seconded to the Lancashire Fusiliers.

This poem is one scenario of many reflecting the military tradition

Father to Son

From Ulster stock and Ulster's soil
Another to soldier, fight and toil
Of that Great War he was the child
Born to a woman meek and mild

His Father, a warrior true and brave
Fought in France beyond the wave
Showing no fear, he fell with his gun
Just days before his son's life begun

Looking on the child with love and smiles
Mother thought of his Father, across the miles
In the son she saw a part of him
A living reminder as her eyes grew dim

Growing up she told him who he was
To think of his Father and sometimes pause
She spoke of War in reverent tone
Careful to neither, condemn or condone

The boy she taught, be modest and proud
Be prepared to act, but never loud
In nineteen thirty nine, he heard the call
'Enlist! Enlist!' was the cry to all

Father in mind, he accepted the shilling
Ready to fight and more than willing
He told his Mother and heard her cry
For a fleeting moment, he wondered why

But he knew, he was all she had
A Mother's reason, for being sad
Preparing to sail from his native shore
"Take care my son", she did implore

He went away and fought the Hun
With bayonet, grenade and blazing gun
Returning home after six long years
To jubilant cries and joyful tears

19.1.96

A Jumble of Thoughts

We are the men and women of the RUC
Always around for others to see

We have stood on Derry's Walls
And done the beat on Belfast's Falls

We held the line at Butchers Gate
From early morn, till the hour was late

We stood and watched the Army come in
Some to never again, see their kith and kin

We have cleared streets in Newry Town
Before the bombs blew buildings down

We have lain in fields around Forkhill
As violent men, tried our blood to spill

We have flown in 'Choppers' with soldier men
Over hill, the vale and Crossmaglen

We have seized pigs at the 'Gap of the North'
As smugglers quietly brought them forth

We have stood in Belfast's City Centre
Facing Catholic, Protestant and Dissenter

We have done our duty and recall
Many a poll count, in the City Hall

We have rubbed shoulders with the SAS
And dealt with those of every class

We have watched the Godfathers strut and boast
All over the World, from coast to coast

We have drank the Devil's brew poteen
And for days after, were not to be seen

We prosecuted men, for illegal slaughter
Their names we forget, nor does it matter

We have sometimes had to fire our gun
Lucky to go home when the day was done

We have watched as some for position clamoured
Who when done down, were not enamoured

We have been up against the barricades
And saw thousands passing in parades

We have seen many a bloody murder
Or serious injury, from disorder

We saw hijackers at their criminal best
And with riot gun, put them to the test

We have seen kerb crawlers by the score
Who although harassed, came back for more

We have found those, who preferred suicide
Intent this World to no longer abide

We have heard murderers, their deeds confess
And through repentance, seek the Lord to bless

We have helped old and young across the road
In keeping with the policeman's code

We have watched men served lots of drink
Money taken, until they were on the brink

We have then heard, the anxious call for police
Get him out of here, before he disturbs the peace

We have for years looked, for bombs under the car
Down on our knees upon the tar

We have heard the gunfire sound
And seen the dead upon the ground

We have noted politicians, jockey for position
Scoring points for some, their only mission

We have seen the arrival of Ministers imported
Skilled and fluent, but not locally supported

We have heard the phrase, "I can categorically say"
Usually heralding lies, with Hell to pay

We have seen men of natural mettle
Slandered by those of lesser fettle

We have heard Clergymen, lament and complain
Saying prayers for the dead and those in pain

We know people, who with every excuse to hate
Forgave their tormentors and accepted their fate

We know those who went to wreck and burn
Causing hardship and strife at every turn

We know neighbours, who failed to extradite
Not through reason, but from spite

We have heard them use, every excuse
To justify the crime, ignore the abuse

We hear those who perceive, history with a slant
Giving themselves the excuse, to rave and rant

We have watched politicians, block the highway
And protest like mad when swept away

We have heard the murderous bullets flit by
And explosions or fires light up the sky

We have seen the coming semblance of peace
Whilst watching the peoples hopes increase

We are aware of some, who supposedly know it all
When it came to security, they never answered the call

We now see them, in positions of power
Spouting from their, individual tower

We realise that this is how things are done
It is after all better, than the way of the gun

20.1.96

The Long Black Coat

Away back in the days of yore
Police wore coats down to the floor
Meant to cover from calf to neck
Weren't really warm and always slack

At the Depot in a line you did stand
Where a coat was handed to every man
"Put them on", the Sergeant did say
We all remember that far off day

Some were up and some were down
Not allowed to laugh, it made you frown
A yardstick was then produced
The long black coats, were to be reduced

Height from the ground was made fourteen
The transformation had to be seen
Not able to get us level at the neck
They made us the same height from the deck

But with the coming modern trend
They've given us coats of a different blend
The rain is now sure to hit your feet
As you go about your daily beat

27.9.95

The Exile

Here I am on a Chilean shore
I know I'll wander this World no more
I've had my three score years and ten
That time allotted to mortal men

There is no doubt I'll soon expire
I feel my limbs and body tire
In my mind I see a place
To the north, which I now face

It is the Town of old Glenarm
A place of magic and of charm
The Vennel, Altmore, Mark and Toberwine
Those little streets, I remember fine

Around these places I used to run
When just a boy, in pursuit of fun
I was hunted by Lord Antrim's men
Whilst poaching salmon in his glen

There is a fairytale castle there
With rounded turrets in the air
Oh! to be in that place, where I was born
At this time as I feel forlorn

I left it oh, so long ago
But I've always missed it so
I know as in this shack I lie
That I am frail and about to die

My spirit then will rise above
And fly like Noah's snowy dove
To old Glenarm, for one last look
Before God opens, his great book

21.2.96

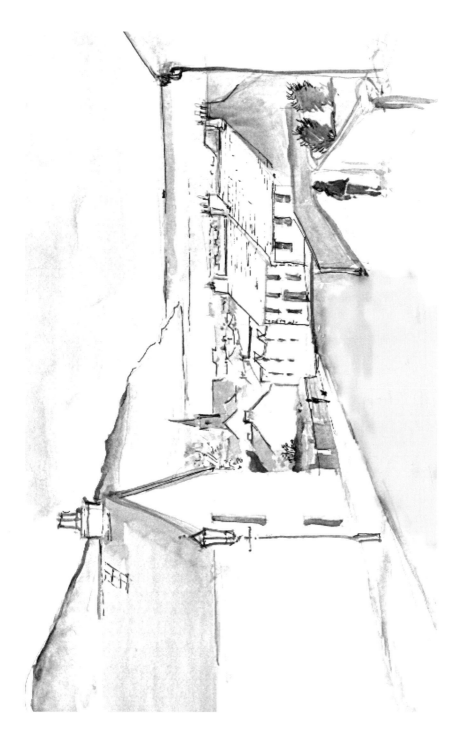

A Casualty of War

R.H.A. No 20683

A Trooper was Tom Cammock, in the Royal Horse Artillery
Who faced the Boer and German, far across the sea
Riding on the lead horse, with cannon behind the team
A little man fulfilling, everyone's heroic dream

Bullet, shell or sabre, never found this Ulster son
It was the germ Malaria, that took him from his gun
Having fought in Africa and managed to survive
Was years after sent to France and still remained alive

But there the Foeman got him, by devious means alas
Using the putrid killer, known as Mustard Gas
With bandaged eyes he left, that bloody battlefield
A half blinded future, fate for him had sealed

As a boy I watched him, shuffling along by the Gasworks wall
That unsung little Hero, who one time rode so tall
Shoulders raised to take more air, in lungs seared long before
He'd seen his days of glory and drove the horse no more

He dwelt for thirty years and more, at his Belfast abode
In the Street of Havelock, just off the Ormeau Road
With his wounds he suffered, the years filled with pain
Until the Lord called him home, a life not lived in vain

Viewing those marching Veterans and on hearing the bugle call
I see Trooper Cammock on the lead horse, mounted proud and tall
In conflict as a youth and man, on a foreign field
Emblazoned in his nature, to not give way or yield

21.11.96

The Diplock Court

At Belfast's Crumlin Road Court, number one
Through those high windows, peeps the winter sun

Sitting in the dock, are the men accused
Looking sombre and not amused

Suit and tie their mode of dress
Calculated, the Learned Judge to impress

Court officials rushing here and there
Some are women, young and fair

Barristers in their cloaks of black
Wigs on their heads, with tails at the back

Surrounded by papers and assorted books
Selected for brains, not their looks

Prison Officers' cap peaks down on their noses
Lounging back in quiet reposes

Relatives in the gallery at the rear
Some under the weather, full of yesterday's beer

Theirs to observe, through a bullet-proof screen
Participants in, this High Court scene

The Tip'staff says, "Everyone rise"
Up jump all, the accused and the wise

The Judge he enters and takes his place
Ready to hear and adjudge this case

It is a procedure that has to be seen
The Tip'staff finishing with, "God Save The Queen"

Now the Judge is resplendent, in his cloak of red
With a white fitted wig upon his head

His collar starched and brilliant white
Truly a serene and marvellous sight

Police in positions, standing all around
Whispers and shuffling, the only sound

The Judge then says, "Gentlemen proceed"
And the Crown Prosecutor gets up to lead

He tells a tale of wanton woe
In rounded tones, precise and slow

With glasses on, he looks up and down
The learned incumbent, representing the Crown

Voice rising and falling, with flourish and flair
Choosing his words, with thought and care

Then to be heard, council for the defence
Their indignation appears immense

"My Lord these allegations we dispute
And with balanced argument can refute

The charges as stated we must contest
For our clients', we'll, proceed with zest"

Witnesses called under oath, one by one
Tedious examination of each, till the day is done

Some are experts, plain to see
Others are people of low degree

The Judge a refinement, of the Public School
Selected for astuteness and nobody's fool

His mind one sees through the evidence steers
Listening to people from different spheres

A witness dressed in a denim coat
Devoid of necktie or collar at his throat

He surveys the Judge with steady stare
As Barristers pick his evidence bare

Judge or witness, as they proceed under law
Each of the other, is in no state of awe

The truth begins to slowly unfold
Defendants go pale, as their blood runs cold

And so it goes on, day after day
As evidence before the Judge they lay

Barristers hypothetically, questioning some
Knowing the kind of evidence, yet to come

In order to cancel, some still obscure point
And with credibility, their clients' anoint

Having heard all the evidence, the Judge, he speaks
"I have assessed the evidence over past weeks

Gentlemen, the evidence against the accused is stout
But I base my decision on, 'beyond reasonable doubt'

My judgement is that I must acquit
On all the charges within the Queen's writ"

Gasps are heard and a woman's cry
Somebody shouts, "The bastards will die"

The public gallery, to order is called
One sees the problem, has not been solved

The acquitted are hurriedly, from sight removed
Their innocence to some, has not been proved

Then on the Courthouse steps, the World to face
They state, "There is no justice in this place"

17.3.96

Revisited

Here I stand in this old school yard
and think of yesteryear
Echoes from the past within my head
as I wipe away a tear

I feel the presence of long ago
at this familiar scene
Surrounded by giant beeches
and fields of emerald green

The old School House is still here
well built in granite stone
But no longer are there children
and now it stands alone

That great oak door is still in place
on ornamented hinge
Wooden eaves above look down
with carved and fretted fringe

Here I'd sit below the trees
and eat my little meal
Then gather up the beech nuts
which I did gently peel

But my clearest recollection
is that first eventful day
My Sister led me to the door
and I didn't want to stay

Gone now are all the children
and the Master is at rest
It is only now I know
having been here, I was blest

18.4.96

Rest Assured

As I wandered along that old highway
To my home at the end of the day

I saw the Church, with its heavenward spire
Behind it the Sun, that celestial fire

Silhouetted over the graveyard wall
Were granite markers, ornate and tall

This scene before me, in just a blink
I became aware and began to think

Of all those people once as I
Behind that wall, there to lie

Awaiting the Judgement, as they must
Decay reducing their forms to dust

I could see those beings in my dream
In life both of high and low esteem

Remembered by tombstones, small and great
Some none at all, or of lowly slate

There lies my friend, 'Old John' the tramp
A gentleman of the road, in sun and damp

Now no material wealth had he
As he ate my food, it was plain to see

But he was rich within his mind
Of Earth's adornment, he was not blind

Also laid there, near him beside
Is a man I knew, of wealth and pride

Of Nature's mantle, he was unaware
And the poor or needy, he didn't care

With his cunning and treachery complete
He felt fulfilled, success was sweet

Now there they lie, in the same estate
Of who was the better, there's no debate

It must be him, who trod the road
And sometimes called, at my abode

5.5.96

Orphan of Rathlin

There is a place that I adore
It lies to the north of a northern shore

Surrounded by a rolling sea
That beckons through my dreams to me

Oh Rathlin, I miss your rugged scene
Tis many years since I have been

Upon the land where I was born
To welcome the arrival, of the morn

I left you as an orphan boy
As famine all life did destroy

With grip of steel, I held the oar
As tears welled up within my core

Moving away in that open boat
I felt the sadness in my throat

Pulling the oar, less time to think
And then you were gone, in just a blink

As rain and mist, rolled across the sea
Putting a blind, between you and me

I was lost and devoid of hope
With not a thought, how I would cope

At first I wanted to return
Fear drove me on and you to spurn

I remained with our lowly band
And we sailed to a far off land

Where I grew up, strong as a tree
On the other side of the Atlantic sea

It was my role, to succeed and prosper
But it is my boyhood that I foster

And to my children, I relate
Those far off days and our fate

It is to Rathlin Isle I yearn
To stand beside, my Mother's cairn

2.2.95

The Cease-Fire

I sit and ponder this new found peace
There are prayers that it will last
Some say its on a short term lease
With 'Partition' not consigned to the past

The men of violence bask in praise
They really feel fulfilled
Decent folk in a bit of a daze
Reflect on the people killed

In this land of Ulster
There must be common ground
Eliminating 'with gun' to muster
Surely a solution can be found

But remember they nailed to a cross
The only one who was ever right
And the Irish to show they're not at a loss
May each other continue to fight

30.9.94

The Round Tower

The rounded tower upon the hill
With its mortared wall
An imposing structure still
A symbol to us all

Of ancestors long since past
Who walked this sacred land
When the Invader's net was cast
To defend they took a stand

Here they faced the Viking
And withstood the Dane
As many a day was breaking
They fought those out for gain

I hear their cries from long ago
At the tower on the hill
Forever fighting a savage foe
Their spirits are there still

14.7.96

A Dell I Know

Travelling along to Crawfordsburn
you'll come on Nature's bower

Where ivy and buttercups abound
and trees above them tower

Here and there one also sees
the subtlety of the fern

Clinging to the mossy banks
or protruding from a cairn

At its given time a shimmering sea
of blue and delicate bell

Another wistful adornment
to hold you in its spell

The oak, the beech and chestnut
touch in profusion there

And just like Eden's garden
a place unique and rare

To see it at its most sublime
is in early morning light

When sunbeams of silver penetrate
a glorious stunning sight

Year by year the seasons flow
over our beloved land

To watch Earth's changing mantle
tis at Crawfordsburn I'll stand

2.6.96

TO THE FALLEN AND THOSE WHO SERVED
ULSTER DEFENCE REGIMENT 1970 - 1992

and my friend

SERGEANT MAJOR KENNETH WISHART (DEC'D)
7/10 (CITY OF BELFAST) BATTALION

You of the Flying Angel Harp, surmounted by the Crown
Patrolled this land of Ulster, from Foyle to the Coast of Down

No civic tablet, it has been decreed, will ever bear your name
Stalwart soldiers do not grieve, your memorial is your fame

Some of you were young and lithe, with others of middle age
It has been your place in history, to write a glorious page

Steadfast you held the line, in this green and northern land
Against the forces of treachery, you chose to take a stand

You did not stop to reason, on the dangers you would face
When you volunteered to serve, upon this soil we all embrace

In the Churchyards of this Country and the Cemeteries of Belfast Town
We can see the granite markers, displaying your Harp and Crown

There they lie awaiting, the 'Trumpet Call' once more
When they'll rally to the colours, as they did in days before

All ye who would deny them, in shame hang down your head
And remember those valiant comrades, now ranked among the dead

21.5.96

The Travel Trunk

I am an old dusty trunk
Sitting on the floor
Out of sight, in the dark
Behind the attic door

Lost, disused or hidden away
I was never meant to be
Having travelled across the World
And sailed on every sea

I was always needed
When Empire was a rising star
Built by clever craftsmen
Who knew I'd travel far

My innards made of seasoned wood
All lined with linen cloth
Every chink accounted for
To keep out the roving moth

With robust outer casing
Of armour good and strong
To protect me from abuse
So nothing would go wrong

Iron rivets all around
And Sheffield steel encased
Dove-tailed along with strips of oak
Is how I am embraced

All those times left waiting
On a far flung dock
My contents well protected
With a good mortise lock

Treasures they were placed in me
And I've graced many a room
Was carried up the Khyber Pass
Later abandoned in Khartoum

No matter where just left to sit
Or in a corner lain
There were always those goin' roamin'
And I'd be on my way again

In the hold of sailing ships
Or tied down on the deck
Davy Jones's locker looming
Not knowing if I'd be back

Then those dirty salt caked coasters
With chugging forward thrust
Floating mountains of iron ore
And engines fit to burst

I have been the yoke of porters
And coolies by the score
Until their legs grew weary
Strained to the very core

I have stored many items
Including uniforms of red
For Queen Victoria's soldiers
Who are long gone and dead

Those days are all departed
With my journeys over
Never again to face salt spray
Or disembark at Dover

Oh! if only I could talk
The stories I would tell
Of war with siege and danger
Right into the jaws of Hell

So if you ever find me
A relic from the past
Remember I've served my time
Over this World so vast

Although forlorn and somewhat worn
With my travelling future bleak
Put me out on display
For your friends who love antique

Don't just stand there looking
At me sitting on the floor
With my reinforced binding
Behind the attic door

1.8.96

In The Shadow of
Tully Castle

I stand upon this reeded shore
at the Lough of Erne

And see the Heron's graceful rise
followed by the Tern

The Sun in the west is sinking
with the water a lustre sea

To the wind the sail boat bends
weaving its way to the lee

Silhouetted on a wooded hill
is a stone built Castle of old

Reminding me of times gone by
and fearsome stories told

The Fisherman patiently waiting
on his prey from the deep

As the Jackdaw rests its weary wing
within the Castle Keep

I see those scattered islands
ever so lush and green

With the Swan and Mallard resting
from all the places they've been

Another day is closing
upon the Lough of Erne

The trees a'quivering in the breeze
with iris, rush and fern

6.7.96

The Widow

Here I rest with eyes closed
our child plays at my feet
As I reflect to youths first flush
in repose upon this seat

The home is neat and tidy
only toys across the floor
From the shadows of my dream
I hear him coming to the door

Remembering back to when we met
on that Summer morn
As he patrolled the Village Street
with love my heart was torn

A glance from him as I passed by
then our eyes met
He said, "Hello", as I smiled
our destiny was set

So he courted and romanced me
with tenderness and care
And after a time we married
at the Church in the Village Square

A joyous event for everyone
was our wedding day
But as beknown it heralded
him being sent away

To patrol in other places
and many an Ulster vale
To face dangers lurking there
each day a stirring tale

Behind the door of our abode
a silent prayer I'd say
To keep him free from harm
each hour and every day

Then one afternoon in autumn time
he did not appear
Seeing his colleagues at the gate
I was filled with fear

Looking up at them in turn
then to each face again
I saw the strain and anguish
keeping in check the pain

With awkwardness they told me
how he'd met his end
There was nothing they could do
death you cannot mend

I hear the hour upon the bell
in the old Church Clock
With it a fleeting glimpse in time
of me in my wedding frock

Now fully awake from my slumber
I've dreamt him at the door
My eyes are misting with sadness
he'll never come home anymore

As I lift our child to embrace him
placing him down on my knee
He laughs and I long for my Husband
the Father, he'll never see

28.8.96

Clannaboye

From Bangor out to Strickland's Glen
Hillocks and rocks abound
A place to hear Nature's overture
In a blend of earthly sound

Smooth pebbles on a rugged shore
Ground down by relentless seas
Descending banks of bramble and fern
With interspersed ancient trees

Contorted and bent by cutting wind
In shapes of one in pain
Bark worn and foliage burned
From salt filled seaborne rain

Twisted weed torn from the depths
Piled around Smelt Mill Bay
Eye catching blackened adornment
In natural sublime array

One day just there as dusk befell
I saw the ghost of Conn O'Neill
In woven cloak, clasped at the throat
Covered from head to heel

These are my lands, his look implied
A Warrior Chief of old
Back at Clannaboye claiming his own
A leader by treachery sold

His phantom figure, not at rest
Roams o'er brake and briar
Surveying a birthright bestowed on him
His spirit does not tire

2.11.96

Freedom

Into slavery born was I
To remain as such, till I would die

The Master gave me clothes for my back
With roof over my head, a wooden shack

Among other things, I got enough food
So that I would work as hard as I could

There I'd be in the fields of cotton
Working away with my roots forgotten

Then the men in the north, a war they fought
Because I was owned and working for naught

Suddenly me and my brothers were free
The first time ever, since crossing the sea

But I'm still here in these cotton fields
Gathering in the yearly yields

Earning the dollars to buy my corn
And my body with clothes adorn

For my shack, I now pay rent
Sometimes I can't, with my money spent

So life goes on, day after day
For whatever I want, I have to pay

I'm earning enough for my basic need
Paid by the Boss, in his thrifty greed

The way I see, nothing much has changed
Since my freedom was arranged

30.3.96

The Victim

A barbarous tale I have to tell
About a man I once knew well

He worked machinery upon the land
Moving earth and sometimes sand

The telephone rang in old Forkhill
To answer politely was the drill

The caller told me who he was
Going on to say without pause

About the man he had last seen
Being led away from his machine

By two men, one with a gun
"Oh! come quick, what have they done

From the highway I heard a shot
Near the cross-roads is the spot"

We hurried out to that place
Suspecting what we had to face

Driving slowly up yonder hill
To a scene, I remember still

I saw that pathetic bundle there
Curled on its side, with sightless stare

Without a doubt, he was dead
A single shot right through his head

As he had wrought within that field
They saw him and his fate was sealed

He was selected to pay with his life
For their bloodlust, in a land of strife

15.4.96

The 75th Anniversary of the Royal British Legion

Standard Bearers to the fore
Holding colours of blue and gold
Representing a family of nations
And their warriors bold

The seventy-fifth year of the Legion
At the Royal Albert Hall
Colonnaded balconies of people
Reflecting the epic call

To defend against an aggressor
And support all those oppressed
Prompted by this calling
With zeal they were possessed

Standing here in the autumn of life
Somewhat tired, but ever so proud
As the Sovereign takes her place
Overlooking this glorious crowd

Medals sparkle, glint and glisten
On those with snowy hair
Fanfares sound in clarion call
Mustering the chosen there

First the intrepid Mariners
In navy with hats of white
Then pith helmeted Royal Marines
A precise and disciplined sight

Marching men in tunics of scarlet
With bearskins on the head
Successors of others before them
The wounded and the dead

Closely followed by plumes of green
The Irish are on parade
Loyal Soldiers of the Crown
Their fame does not fade

Men and women from every service
Go forth to their appointed place
Also the Chelsea Pensioners
At a slow and dignified pace

Wearing the three cornered hat
Dressed in coats of red
Honours festooning each breast
None braver it could be said

Now berobed and mitred Clergy
To bestow blessings and give thanks
On the lowered Standard
And those of various ranks

The skirl of Highland Pipers
Whilst colleagues dance the sword
A sound heard by enemies past
As many a cannon roared

Welshmen in choral harmony
In voices high and low
Pursuing their great tradition
As sweet melodies flow

Continuity orderless marching
That others could not match
By those wearing Air Force blue
Exact as any watch

Throughout this solemn encounter
Trumpet, piccolo and drum beat
To enthral all those present
With performers at their feet

Hymns are sung, an address is said
The 'Last Post', it is played
Poppies cascading on the young
Thoughts of the valiant dead

At the last a kettledrum roll
Preceding, 'God Save The Queen'
Thus ending all the homage
Remembered by those who have been

Poppies lie in abundance
Having fallen down like rain
A reminder to the living
Of the blood, spilled on the plain

12.11.96

Fruit of Depression

I think of times long ago
And sometimes feel, I can say 'Hello'

To people who were once as I
But time ran out and had to die

In my dreams I see my Father's face
Across the divide in another place

In his steps I may follow
Over mountain top and yonder hollow

I feel vibrations in the air
And wonder is there someone there

Looking after me from day to day
As I work, sleep, hope and pray

Time goes by and the years pile on
It seems remote, since my dawn

When I wandered to the country school
To read and write as was the rule

Treacherous men they me frustrate
And I respond with latent hate

Which tends to irritate the soul
Like a fire within from burning coal

I strive to treat all men as equal
Realising there is no sequel

To the daily thrust and grind
In this life which tends to bind

But we owe, to those now stilled
To face life's hazards and be fulfilled

2.10.95

Rambling Rose

Oh, rambling rose I see you grow
in profusion through the hedge
I watch you weave to seek a place
at every nook and mortared ledge

Abundantly your buds appear
like little green drops of dew
Proclaiming forthcoming scarlet rosettes
blossoms for all to view

Then you'll bask in proud display
on vantage points facing the Sun
Along the hedge and up over the wall
everywhere your tentacles run

The days must pass and your petals fall
upon the Earth like rain
I'll look at you as your glory fades
with your foliage plain again

The miracle of your creation
was adornment meant to be
For you to entwine, seek out or find
and bring joy to the Honey Bee

So some you sustain, with the nectar of life
in your prime for us to observe
Year after year, you bring pleasure to man
and the creatures that you serve

5.12.96

The Patriot

When just a boy I stood there
At my Mother's knee

Beaming down into my face
She said a Patriot I would be

She told me heroic stories
Of times long ago

When Ireland's sons fought for her
Against a savage foe

I learned the language of the Gael
Being our mother tongue

Everyone was proud of me
Moreso as I was young

I always knew of Sarsfield's ride
Through the dark of night

To spike the Williamite guns
Before the coming fight

I read about that glorious stand
Back in nineteen sixteen

Had I been alive then
That's where I would have been

Growing up a young man
In this northern state

Knowing Ireland's history
With venom I did hate

All those men not as I
The Forces of the Crown

Dressed in green and khaki
Patrolling Belfast Town

It was just then that I perceived
For it to be my fate

To fight these cursed foreigners
And them eradicate

So I was sworn to soldier
For old Ireland's cause

To aim for total victory
And never stop or pause

With enthusiasm I listened
And learned my bloody trade

In striking blows for Ireland
Others were in the shade

I used the bomb and bullet
Fired from the sniper's gun

Proud was I a soldier
My Mother's Patriot son

Then one night as I did sleep
They came and captured me

Breaking the door of my abode
Before I could shoot or flee

Reflecting now on past years
In this prison cell

Baptised in fire but now mature
A story I must tell

In this place are Orangemen
Prisoners of their kind

They're Irishmen just like me
To this I'm no longer blind

It is to them I now relate
In our common plight

And a shame that we ever
Each other had to fight

So when you speak to children
Avoid talk of all past wrong

Teach them with care and wisdom
Wherever they belong

Patriotism is fine and well
A dream within your head

Don't do as I have done
With people maimed and dead

6.4.96

Return to Rathlin

As a wide eyed boy I listened
To the stories often told

Of a far flung rugged island
Around which the ocean rolled

My Father wistfully remembering
How it was his native home

Away from the coast of Maine
Beyond the Atlantic foam

"My boy these things I speak of
You remember well

And when you are a man full grown
To others you must tell

Of the isle that gave me life
That gem in a northern sea

Where in life and death
My heart will always be"

Now I grew up and roamed the Earth
This lore within my head

I sailed on 'Yankee' clipper ships
And to foreign lands have sped

Father's tales a spur to me
When danger I had to face

"Your blood is of that Rathlin stock
A sound and hardy race"

Then one day as we sailed west
On a fierce and turbulent sea

We ran for a sheltered anchorage
In a welcome island lee

Seeing those white cliffs, capped with black
From that placid bay

A familiar feeling came to me
I remember to this day

That little Church with square built tower
The houses low and white

With Rathlin Isle before me
A haunting awesome sight

On headlands standing all around
Yellow ochre of the whin

Always remembered by my Sire
When he grew old and thin

No mighty pines stood there
As in my native Maine

Moreso the sloping stunted thorn
Bent by wind and rain

There I stood enraptured
Until the day was dark

Father still upon my mind
From this place so stark

Then there at the break of day
To herald the coming morn

We weighed and stowed our anchor
And left the land, where he was born

9.6.96

A Message to the Gunman

You'll be at the appointed place
The next target intent to kill

At times information supplied to you
From those who wish them ill

Always justifying your actions
In the cause that you believe

Oblivious of tragic suffering
By those just left to grieve

You've scarred this land with foul deeds
And were many a man's death knell

The Widow's grief and Orphan's curse
Will follow you to Hell

24.6.96

The Demise of Bangor Bay

The realigned face of Old Bangor
Up at the top of Down
Hardly a sight from the past
In this resort of esteem and renown

Still in place, the old sea wall
But the Bay is no longer there
All those yachts and jetties
I could only stand and stare

Also the sign for Pickie Pool
Upon that eternal rock
Gone as well the pool itself
To which we used to flock

No coal from blackened Puffers
Being piled high on the quay
Where the little boats took their rest
From ventures on the sea

Or encrusted wooden stanchions
Supporting a rickety pier
An excellent place to fish from
By men and boys with their gear

Then said I to a passer-by
If I could hire a boat from Laird
He looked at me with a wistful smile
They were gone and I hadn't heard

On sauntering along by that old wall
I saw the McKee Municipal Clock
Impressive and tall as it ever was
Made from precision cut sandstone block

Still to be admired is the Harbour House
With its old square cornered tower
From which were observed the Windjammers
Later Steamers with pressurised power

All one sees now is a boatyard
And craft stripped ready for paint
With stainless steel fittings and halyards
There's no sign of anything quaint

So I turned on my heel in an instant
Going back the way I had come
It is hard to accept all the changes
I suppose its all right for some

They developed a natural feature
With a civic idea of fun
Obliterating all in the process
Around which we used to run

Then I was back at the old sea wall
With its wave rutted copes of stone
As a reminder of another time
It ruggedly stands alone

21.8.96

The Ballylesson Blacksmith

A Forge of repute was Sandy Gray's
At Fort Road below Purdysburn Hill
Where that Magician in steel and the shaping of iron
Displayed the Blacksmith and Farrier's skill

Taking metal white hot, straight out of the fire
Held in tongs that were ancient and worn
On the anvil he'd hammer, with sharpness of eye
Heat and sparks he treated with scorn

Whether axle or blade, pitchfork or spade
He repaired and made them all
The Farmer demented, with yoke bent or broke
Thought of Sandy and gave him a call

Flat bar into hoops, their ends welded by fire
Beat together until they were one
Placed over cart wheels, down on the ground
Shrunk by water, is how it was done

Tools he would temper, in fire and in oil
With a touch on the old grinding wheel
Making them sharp, with a good cutting edge
To test, with his thumb he would feel

Now pivotal gates were much to his taste
Along with scrolls and some fleur-de-lis
Ironwork in the Church, by the skill of his hand
Remains there for all to see

As a boy that Smithy was heaven to me
With its bellows and fire so bright
Six horses or more in a line to be shod
Real horsepower, what a wonderful sight

Now Sandy a man of temperate mood
The horse he could calm and entice
He'd back up a Hunter with flight in its eye
And off its worn shoes he would prise

I watched him manoeuvre with pony and shire
A fetlock raised up from the ground
To bed it well in, a burning shoe to the hoof
Then quenched, nailed and filed all around

As a man I saw that Blacksmith Shop
With Sandy no longer there
The fire it was cold, at the heart of the Forge
Where he had toiled with talent and flair

The anvil lay silent, no longer to ring
Sitting inside on the floor
Implements from the past, some rusted and red
Were propped to the side of the door

That haven of quaint industrious skill
Is now superseded by time
Remember the Maestro, whose realm it was
With his work and design sublime.

6.12.96

Pay Heed

With tools of destruction, you ride forth in might
To overcome Ulster by sorrow and fright
Oh, foolish assailant, do you not see
Only through friendship, can you win over me

Killing and scorching, your damnedest have done
Ignoring plea and lament , against murder and gun
You talk of occupied Ireland and fill it with death
I'll counter you and your cadre, to my final breath

Godfather, Assassin and young Volunteer
Come away from your struggle and spare me the tear
Let the salve of our friendship, heal and unite
To resolve distrust and hatred, us no longer to fight

Advocates of concern, with the bovine stare
A disguise for the Wolf, in its hungry lair
Aside with your bitterness and feelings inbred
Try to nurture, the common ground, instead

Let us look to the future, where our children belong
Not to the past, in saga and song
All ye who oppose us, hear this my plea
Only unbridled friendship, can ever win me

29.12.96

Star of Bethlehem

(Campanula isophylla)

Within the perpetual passage of time
As the Creator surveyed his plan
He knew that the day had come
For his Son to descend as Man

Above the birthplace to hover a Star
Never seen or shown before
To herald the King's arrival
Now told in ancient lore

My existence is a living sign
A symbol to great and small
Of that celestial diadem
So you can recall

Named for the 'Star Of Bethlehem'
My flowers are pure and white
To remind you of the 'Christ Child'
In the Manger's gentle light

Place me on a window sill
Where I'll always face the Sun
Through each day of every month
As the seasons run

A garland of profusion
Is my gift by God's decree
Heart shaped leaves in abundance
With blooms for all to see

5.2.97

In Bangor's Ward Park, County Down, is a German Submarine gun from U.B.19, to commemorate the exploits of Commander, the Hon. Edward Barry Stewart Bingham RN who won the Victoria Cross at the Battle of Jutland on the 31st May 1916.

He was rescued from the sea by the German Navy after his ship HMS Nestor was sunk and remained a prisoner of war until 1918. He became a Rear Admiral and died at London in 1939.

This poem reflects on the gun itself, circumstances surrounding it and Lieutenant Commander Otto Weddigen of the Imperial German Navy, who inflicted serious losses on the British Royal Navy, whilst in command of submarines. Lieutenant Commander Weddigen did not survive the war and perished with his crew in U.B.29 after having attacked the British Grand Fleet on the 25 March 1915 as it returned to Scapa Flow.

The Gun

A Cannon of battles long in the past
Engineered and rifled its death to cast
Accoutrements missing, with vacant breech
Quadrants calibrated, to measure its reach

Twas never meant a trophy to be
The spoil of war for the foe to see
Anchored now on its plinth of stone
Shells on the sea, long since sown

This naval piece, from U.B. Nineteen
That iron fish, both sleek and mean
Challenged the might, of the Royal Navy
From beneath our northern sea

A Captain of such menace below
Observed three cruisers, unaware and slow
Clearing torpedo tubes, at each in turn
Saw them sink, explode and burn

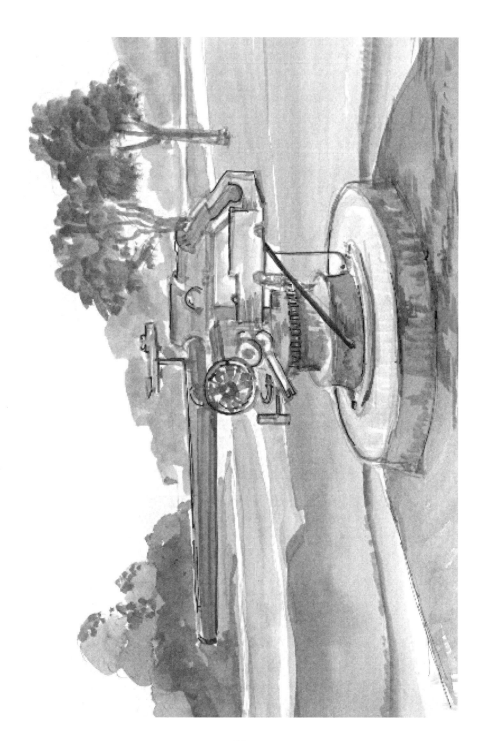

Then a day came, no return from the deep
Commander and crew, in eternal sleep
To serve the Fatherland, never again
Gone was their anguish, fear and pain

A worthy tribute, to a Bangor son
Is one formidable, assailant's gun
Remember those men, in conflict cast
Forever lost, in the mist of the past

26.2.97

Looking North

The swirling waves upon the reef
bubble, froth and beat
A seagull parries with the wind
its feathers sleek and neat
Water thrown against the stone
and repelled in staid disdain
Undeterred from its landward thrust
rushes back again

The Sun arising in the East
to enhance the glistening dew
Its rays seek out the shadows
touching old and new
The rounded contour of the hills
under blue and clouded sky
Between here and Valhalla
where the Nordic Heroes lie

7.2.97

The Pipes

That soil is our soil, the place of our birth
The Highland, the Island, along by the Firth
Piper and Pibroch, the sound of our land
At Culloden and battles, where'er we did stand

Nothing is sweeter than the skirl of the Pipe
On Mountain or Glen, when the barley is ripe
The splash of the Tartan and quivering reed
Are the symbols of Scotland and kindred seed

We've followed its chant and heard the Lament
In foreign fields, where'er we were sent
Across desert sands and the shell holes of Hell
At India's outposts, the Pipes cast their spell

The enemy heard and knew we had come
Raising hopes in near vanquished and terror in some
Who knew the proud sound, of the kilted and brave
Leading kinsmen in strife, to glory or grave

In the lilt of the Pipe and the twirl of the Plaid
One sees Lochs and Islands, roamed as a Lad
Swirling mists of the past, bring a tear to the eye
And we vow to ourselves , to return bye and bye

On America's plains, in Australia's fierce heat
The Bagpipes are, Caledonia's heartbeat
A tingle of pride, is what we all feel
Whether March, a Lament, or old Gaelic Reel

8.6.97

30th November 1995

I stood at Belfast's City hall
And heard the President make the call
To thousands of people gathered there
Addressing them with panache and flair
On reasons why the peace should hold
So that in future years it would be told
How reason and tolerance won the day
With tranquillity the state of play
He was supported by people of every hue
Showing respect, which to him was due
They praised him high and praised him low
The truth from him did surely flow
Suddenly there was an unseen chink of light
Beaming forth from left and right
From Ireland's sons and daughters everywhere
Showing the World that they did care
Joining their voices together as one
To overcome bullet, bomb and the gun
The violent men skulking in their lair
They could not appreciate or share
The groundswell of opinion against their kind
Like everything else, to this they're blind
But they know in their heart of hearts
Its woe betide to him that starts
To break this fragile new-found peace
Being distilled as peoples hopes increase
BILL CLINTON, Mr President, we must say
Thanks for everything, you carried the day

6.12.95

90

For Diana – Princess of Wales

The Lily of the Valleys, is broken, plucked and gone
No longer will her perfect form, walk the World upon

Far up in the cosmos, million miles past the Sun
A Star is shinning brightly, for her life now run

The Casket it was draped, with the Lions of our land
Hibernia's Harp included and flanked by scarlet band

No drumbeat in the morning air, just the sobbing crowd
And the crunch of carriage wheel, with the hoofbeat loud

There they stood in reverence, stunned as it moved along
Gun Carriage, sombre accolade, a symbol to that throng

Here was a Queen within their hearts, at the measured pace
Of the Guard and Postillion high, all of solemn face

Worthy Champion for the afflicted, a woman of regal fame
Followed by a cortege, of infirm, sick and lame

No greater homage could be paid, to such a Rose so fair
Revered by those of every race, for sincerity with flair

We saw her of the twinkling eye, carefree as a girl
Followed there by those in grief, four Princes and an Earl

Then the toll of the muffled bell, from the belfry high
For the one taken away, whom we didn't want to die

Recited poems, with lessons read, songs and talk of love
In honour of her lying there, and the Lord above

Applause heard in London Town, rippled through the door
Carried on a spreading wave, across that stone cut floor

Spontaneous, sincere approval, for all that had been said
About that Lily of the Valleys, whose precious life had fled

Then to the island in the lake, trees reflecting on the water
Surrounded by her kith and kin, and the wild birds chatter

Taken from us in an autumn night, she lies a Swan at rest
All who loved and knew her, feel that they've been blest

7.9.97

The Tenth Anniversary
of the
Enniskillen Cenotaph Bombing

They stand together in silent prayer
Candles flickering in the breeze
The old, the young and then unborn
Beside still waters, near autumn trees

Ten years have passed, since that awful day
When Hell's spawn struck a blow
On those remembering a Nation's 'War Dead'
Where the Erne waters flow

The rumbling bang and after shock
With the rubble piled high
The injured numbered sixty three
And eleven were to die

Shadowy silence reigns, o'er all those here
In yellow candle light
As they recall that scurrilous deed
An outrageous terrible sight

Each dancing flame, proclaims to all
Memories of those who fell
Deep are the thoughts, of the assembled here
Now encroached by the tolling bell

A sea of faces, captures the mood
As many a tear is shed
Ghosts of the past are in this place
Where Poppies are displayed

Oh, United Irelander, these people command
No glory for your foul deed
You stand condemned and forever damned
By yours and kindred seed

The hopeless goal, you blindly serve
In the carnage that you cause
Do you feel any pride, in your cursed soul
When you reflect or pause

Innocent blood you have spilt, on this ancient soil
Where Saint Patrick, walked with his rod
Forgiveness from some, your conscience may ease
But Judgement, awaits, by our God

8.11.97